S0-EAY-669

Nineteenth Century America

THE
NEWSPAPERS

A NEWSBOY ABOUT 1860

Nineteenth Century America

THE
NEWSPAPERS

written and illustrated by
LEONARD EVERETT FISHER

Holiday House · New York

Library of Congress Cataloging in Publication Data

Fisher, Leonard Everett.
  The newspapers.

  (Nineteenth century America)
  Includes index.
  SUMMARY: Traces the development of newspapers
in the United States during the 19th century and
discusses their role in bringing information to and
shaping the views of a country with a rapidly
growing population, rising literacy rate, and
expanding frontiers.
  1. American newspapers—History—19th century—
Juvenile literature. [1. Newspapers] I. Title.
II. Series.
PN4864.F5   071'.3   80-8812
ISBN 0-8234-0387-4 (lib. bdg.)

List of Illustrations

A COLONIAL PRINTING PRESS USED IN THE EARLY 19th CENTURY

Author's Note

The United States was a new nation in 1787 when Thomas Jefferson, Minister to France, wrote, "The basis of our government being the opinion of the people, the very first object should be to keep that right; and were it left to me to decide whether we should have a government without a newspaper, or newspapers without a government, I should not hesitate to prefer the latter."

A century earlier, the governor of Virginia, William Berkeley, had a different idea about public opinion and the printing press. "Learning has brought disobedience, and heresy, and sects into the world," he stated, "and printing has divulged them, and libels against the best government. God keep us from both."

There were no newspapers in Berkeley's America. There were only a few printers trying to publish religious works, for the most part. Yet Berkeley knew that printed information critical of government could move ordinary citizens to disturb the established order.

Similar fears persisted in the provisional Puritan government of Massachusetts. In 1690, Benjamin Harris tried to publish America's first newspaper, *Publick Occurences,* in Boston, without an official license. The paper disappeared after its first edition.

It mattered little whether or not Berkeley or Puritan Massachusetts sensed the threat and onrush of history. By the time Jefferson had made his "newspaper" remark—a remark seeded in the experience of a successful rebellion—some 35 irregularly published newspapers had sparked the American Revolution, destroying British dominance over the 13 colonies. Among these newspapers were the *Massachusetts Spy,* the *Boston News-Letter,* the *New-England Courant,* the *American Weekly Mercury,* the *New-York Gazette,* the *Pennsylvania Gazette,* the *New-York*

Weekly Journal, and the *Virginia Gazette* (Williamsburg).

Also, in 1787, the young American nation had reached a population of 3,500,000. The *Pittsburgh Gazette* was a year old. And the *Pennsylvania Packet,* America's first successful daily newspaper, was three years old. Twelve years later, in 1796, the Alexandria, Virginia, *Gazette* printed its first edition and became one of the country's oldest continuously published newspapers.

Three years later, in 1799, George Washington, America's symbol of all that was decent and right, was dead. The entire world mourned as Americans everywhere braced themselves for a new century and a new era.

I. 1800-1829

"Most of the citizens of America," wrote newspaper editor Noah Webster in the first edition of *American Minerva* (December 9, 1793), "are not only able to read their native language . . . they have a strong inclination to acquire . . . means of knowledge. Of all these means of knowledge," he continued, "newspapers are the most eagerly sought after, and the most generally diffused. In no other country on earth, not even in Great Britain, are newspapers so generally circulated among the body of people, as in America."

Webster's patriotic enthusiasm for the high quality of American literacy sprang from a city sometimes given over to such excesses—New York. In 1793, New York City was the largest and most densely populated city in America. There, 50,000 inhabitants speaking nearly 20 different languages tried to keep pace with the latest happenings in politics and business. Not all of these people could read English. In fact, many of them could not read in any language, including their own native tongues. It was not until the mid-19th century that compulsory elementary education in free, tax-supported American public schools became a reality. Until then it was mostly the well-to-do who learned to read and write. The rest of the young generations were either left to their own devices or apprenticed to butchers, bakers, iron-mongers, and all those trades and crafts society found useful and necessary. Many of these learned to read and write, but many did not.

Whatever the truth of Noah Webster's observation, and whatever the realities of America's ability to read well, New York City reached the year 1800 with 11 or 12 newspapers being published on a scheduled basis and a vigorous population of 60,000 souls. The rest of the country—16 states, 5 territories,* and the District of Columbia, all east of the Mississippi River—boasted some 190 newspapers and a population of about 5,250,000.

Mississippi, Kentucky, Tennessee and Pennsylvania had their *Gazettes;* Ohio its *Centinel;* and West Virginia its *Guardian.* The places where all these newspapers and more were founded—Natchez, Lexington, Knoxville, Pittsburgh, Cincinnati, and Shepherdstown —were all tiny villages and hardly a dot on a respectable map. Men like John Scull and Joseph Hull set up their small press near a Pittsburgh papermill and printed their *Gazette* for the villagers about every other week, or whenever they had enough paper. Usually, frontier papers like the *Pittsburgh Gazette* printed what information and rumors they could borrow from papers being published in more densely populated areas—in this case, Philadelphia. And if the news was stale in

---

*states: Connecticut, Delaware, Georgia, Kentucky, Maryland, Massachusetts, New Hampshire, New Jersey, New York, North Carolina, Pennsylvania, Rhode Island, South Carolina, Tennessee, Vermont, Virginia

territories: Alabama, Indiana, Maine, Mississippi, Ohio

Philadelphia—a few days old—which was normal, it was even that much more stale in Pittsburgh or anywhere else in America. The gathering of news was not that efficient or quick. Domestic news was sometimes weeks old by the time it was read in a local paper. Foreign news took a month or two to reach an American newspaper.

NEWS ON THE FRONTIER

Much of this "old" news dealt with national politics and income-producing advertisements rather than with local events. Local happenings were known by everyone in town—if it was a small town—before such occurrences could ever reach the printed page of a newspaper. What was important was what was happening to the country and what was going on in Europe, particularly in England, France, and Spain, countries that had significant holdings on the North American continent. Britain may have lost her colonies, but she still possessed Canada. France owned a great swath of land from Louisiana to Montana. And Spain owned Florida together with the Mississippi and Alabama coastline along the Gulf of Mexico.

The death of George Washington on December 14, 1799, was a national event of world-wide importance. Moreover, the death of America's first president and war leader was the last momentous historical event of the 18th century, Although rumors were heard everywhere, the people of Salem, Massachusetts, knew nothing about the death until they read it in their *Gazette* some two weeks later. And the frontier population of Cincinnati, Ohio, had no idea that George Washington had died, until they read about it in their *Centinel* on January 7, 1800.

By 1800, there were more newspapers per capita being published in the city of New York than anywhere else in America. These newspapers, like the *Daily Advertiser,* the *Journal of Commerce,* the *Courier and Enquirer* and the *Mercantile Advertizer,* did not exist for the purpose of spreading news among the ordinary population. These papers and others in the large port cities strung out along the Atlantic seaboard were instruments of business interests and the political community.

News of crimes, wars, revolutions, fires, earthquakes, births, deaths, marriages, sports, and the weather were incidental to the world of politics and business. Human interest stories were not as important as the arrival and departure of merchant ships and the identification of their cargoes—slaves, raw materials, and manufactured products.

NEWS ON THE WATERFRONT

Paid advertisements seeking or offering business and job opportunities or the buying and selling of goods of every description sometimes took up most of the space on the front page of a folded, one-sheet newspaper. Along with the commercial news and advertisements, newspaper readers would usually find various shades of opinion dealing with political activities affecting state and country. Often, editorial criticism was rooted in a newspaper's opposition to a political party in power, rather than connected to fact, circumstance, and reason. The mix of fact, rumor, unfounded reports, misinformation, and nasty politicking together with news gathering techniques that were hardly more than printing what had already appeared in another newspaper made newspapermen vulnerable to attacks by those who deemed themselves publicly ridiculed, insulted, and personally damaged or politically ruined by the press.

The First Amendment to the United States Constitution—"Congress shall make no laws . . . abridging the freedom of speech, or of the press . . ."—did not prevent politicians from hauling editors, publishers, and writers into court on charges of libel. Rightly or wrongly, editors went to jail having been convicted of slandering an office holder. By the same token, politicians were driven from public life by newspaper attacks upon their conduct, opinions, service, and voting records, whatever the truth. At the heart of such legal combat was a search for the truth.

14

A cornerstone of American liberty and freedom of the press had already been established in 1735 when a British court found an American editor, Peter Zenger, publisher of the *New-York Weekly Journal,* not guilty, in a case involving his criticism of the British governor of New York, William Cosby. Zenger, accused of libel, was found innocent of the charge because, reasoned the court, he had told the truth and truth could not be construed as libel. Yet, all during the 19th century American courts were confronted with numerous libel suits growing out of newspaper columns. Time and again judges and juries tried to maintain the freedom of the press and uphold the First Amendment to the United States Constitution while deciding in some case where truth ended, if at all, and where libel began, if libel was indeed committed.

In 1801, the leader of the Democrat-Republican Party, Thomas Jefferson, was elected the third President of the United States. The old Federalist party headed by Alexander Hamilton was fading, but not Hamilton. While Jefferson counted his votes, Hamilton founded the *New York Evening Post.* William Coleman was installed as editor, and America's oldest continuously published daily newspaper was launched for the sole purpose of driving Jefferson and the Democrat-Republicans out of office.

Over the next 28 years, the *Post* not only exercised its political muscle, it also printed commercial news, book reviews, and poetry. By the time William Cullen Bryant became editor in 1829 and changed the paper's political focus by embracing Democrat Andrew Jackson,* the *Post* was being read by some 2,000 New Yorkers. The population of New York City by then had exceeded 125,000.

Between 1801 and 1829, news from abroad was momentous. United States forces had subdued Arab pirates at Tripoli; Great Britain executed Irish patriot Robert Emmet in Dublin; France's Napoleon Bonaparte had come and gone—but not before selling the entire Louisiana Territory to the United States; Venezuela's Simón Bolívar drove the Spanish from South America; Mexico separated herself from Spain; Brazil separated herself from Portugal; and the first steam-driven railroad began operating in England.

At home, during the same period, news was just as momentous. Lewis and Clark explored the vastness of the Northwest; Aaron Burr, Vice President of the United States, killed Alexander Hamilton in a duel; Robert Fulton's steamboat *Clermont* sailed up the Hudson River inaugurating the era of steamships; America went to war with Great Britain once more and won—but not before Washington, D.C., including the White House, was put to the British torch; the Erie Canal opened in New York facilitating the shipping of

---

*The Democratic Party grew out of the earlier Democrat-Republican Party of Thomas Jefferson. It dropped "Republican" from its name with the election of Jackson in 1828.

raw materials from the West into New York City, making the city the financial and shipping capital of the country; and on July 4, 1827, New York State abolished slavery.

All this news and more, however tardily printed, was read first by those who could afford to purchase the paper. Newspapers were bought by subscription, not by individual copy. There were no corner newstands. In large cities like New York where subscriptions cost anywhere from $8 to $12 a year and where newspapers were delivered by mail to the home or business office of the subscriber, the average wage earner, working for $1 a day did not buy a subscription. He or his family or

SUBSCRIPTION DELIVERY

friends read discarded papers or else received news from town criers, travelers, employers, and others.

By 1820, 19th century industrialization had begun to provide steam-driven, cylinder printing presses capable of printing 2,000 papers an hour. There were now between nine and ten million people in America. In 1822, automatic machinery for casting type was introduced. The slow hand setting of type could be eliminated in favor of the speedier process where it concerned newspaper printing. Moreover, papermills were now able to mass produce paper if they had the machinery. And firms such as Wrigley & Johnson in Philadelphia were already producing printing inks in vast quantities.

HOE PRESSES—"ROTARY" 1840's

While the technology was present to mass produce newspapers for the fast growing American society, the newspaper publishers themselves did not produce their papers for the average wage earner. Instead they aimed their papers at the well-to-do politicians, statesmen, merchants, mastercraftsmen, farmers, ship owners and captains, military officers, and industrialists—those who could afford to pay the price of the subscription and who could most profit (or lose) from the information the papers contained. There was no attempt by newspaper publishers to reach the ordinary citizen with commercial news, politics, or the doings of the rest of the world.

On March 4, 1829, however, the body politic of the young United States changed its privileged, upper class direction. Andrew Jackson, born in poverty, took the

"WEB" 1870's

oath of office as the seventh president. A founder of the Democratic Party, Jackson was determined to "let the people rule," a slogan he used during the election campaign. He began by inviting the disorderly throng of frontiersmen and others, who had come to see him inaugurated, into the White House, to enjoy the cheese, cake, and punch. By day's end the interior of the mansion was in a shambles, but Washington society knew that the power base of the lower classes would have to be reckoned with during the Jackson administration, if not in all the other administrations to follow.

JACKSON'S PARTY AT THE WHITE HOUSE

The lessening of the ruling class' influence and the rise of the common man in American society, together with the country's increased industrialization, widened the marketplace for newspapers. Now, with more and more ordinary people coming into positions of political influence, more newspapers would have to be published that would appeal to the general public.

II. 1830-1859

By the time Andrew Jackson began serving his second presidential term in 1833, the steam driven cylinder press which had previously revolutionized the newspaper printing business 13 years before had been improved upon. Inventor Richard Hoe, a New Yorker, had contrived a double cylinder printing press that enabled printers to produce 4,000 papers an hour.

More importantly, in September, 1833, a 20-year-old New York printer from Springfield, Massachusetts, Benjamin H. Day, began publishing a morning newspaper, the *Sun*. He sold it on the streets of New York by the single issue for one penny. The penny paper was not a new idea. It had been tried in other cities only to quickly fail for one lackluster reason or another. The *Sun* persisted, however. It became the first "penny press" paper to succeed. It appealed to many segments of New York society with its variety of information, ranging from financial news to humorous human interest stories—mostly about drunks—extracted from New York Police blotters. Now, newspaper readership would no longer be limited to the privileged few. Newspapers could be mass produced and sold for prices that even the lowest wage earner could afford.

Over the next 17 years, 1833-1850, the "penny press" thrived in the big cities. And there was news enough to fill the pages. America had fought a war with Mexico

and won the southwest territories. Texas had become a
state but not before Davy Crockett and Jim Bowie had
died at the Alamo. Gold was discovered in California.
An American expedition discovered that Antarctica was
a continent. Samuel F. B. Morse had invented the
telegraph. Ether made surgical operations painless for
the first time. The railroad had come to America.
Benjamin Franklin's face appeared on the first adhesive-
backed United States postage stamp.

SAMUEL FINLEY BREESE MORSE

Politically, the country had passed through five presidents during this period: Andrew Jackson, Martin Van Buren, William Henry Harrison, John Tyler and James K. Polk. The industrial North, the agricultural South, the settled East and the unsettled West each sought to protect or expand its own way of life. America, now sectionalized, was on a collision course. Slavery was the immediate issue.

SOLD INTO SLAVERY

News from abroad indicated a fast changing world as well. Revolts were blossoming all over western and central Europe sending a wave of immigrants to the United States. An obscure German philosopher, Karl Marx, and a colleague, Frederick Engels, published *The Communist Manifesto*. And slavery was no longer an issue in Great Britain. It was banned.

All this news and more was delivered in newspapers
—in the "penny press"—that swamped the streets.
During this 17 year period, James Gordon Bennett had
founded the *New York Herald,* a paper devoted to
financial news, sensational crimes, and foreign news,
most of which was written by Bennett himself. In New
Orleans, George Kendall and Francis Lumsden founded
the *Picayune.* In Brooklyn, across the East River from
New York's Manhattan Island, the poet Walt Whitman
had become editor of the recently founded *Brooklyn
Eagle.* Horace Greeley stirred readers with the humani-
tarian flavor of his newly founded New York *Tribune.*
Greeley's *Tribune,* called "the great moral organ," was
the first to establish a regular editorial page in which
the editor, Greeley, commented and gave opinions that
reflected the paper's position on political, economic, and
social affairs. Keen competitors, New York's *Herald*
and *Tribune* would merge in the 20th century to become the *Herald Tribune.*

Chicago, too, would have its *Tribune.* It was founded
in 1847 by John L. Scripps, whose descendants would
later establish a national chain of newspapers bearing
the Scripps name. Also, a *Herald* was founded in Boston
and competed with two earlier newspapers, the
Transcript founded in 1830 and lasting 111 years, and
the *Liberator,* a vehement anti-slavery newspaper,
founded and edited by a 26 year old out-spoken Abolitionist, William Lloyd Garrison, in 1831.

Two problems confronted the burgeoning newspaper industry: the gathering of news and information, and the distribution of newspapers to the public. Until the late 1840's there was little efficiency in these areas.

Here and there, some newspapers employed reporters and correspondents to furnish them with facts regarding various events. Reporters covered Congress while war correspondents traveled with the troops during the Mexican War. Foreign news was brought to newspaper offices by ship captains. Much of this news arrived weeks, sometimes months, after the fact. Telegraphy was new, not widely available, and costly.

Newspapers were not averse to inventing stories to either increase their circulation or to keep their clients busy reading while hard news was on the way. In 1835, the New York *Sun* ran a story about telescopic sightings on the moon. It told of the discovery, by the son of a famous astronomer, of plants and animals on the moon. The tale was backed up with such serious scientific verbiage that everyone believed it, including other newspapers, which took the *Sun's* story and reprinted it. The *Sun's* circulation immediately rose some 5,000 copies, until the fake story was revealed by the man who wrote it, the *Sun's* top writer, Richard Adam Locke.

In order to improve news-gathering, six New York newspapers, the *Sun, Herald, Tribune, Courier and Enquirer, Express,* and *Journal of Commerce* joined together in 1848 to form the New York Associated

ASSOCIATED PRESS REPORTERS AND A TELEGRAPHER

Press. They pooled their resources into one office for the purpose of gathering news, and then selling it to newspapers outside New York City. Instead of six newspapers each trying to file the same story on six separate telegraph lines, the association transmitted one story over one telegraph line which was then dispatched to the six newspapers. The association would then sell the story in Boston, Philadelphia, and other places. Sometimes the stories were sent via carrier pigeons, or by express riders, if telegraphy was not available. In the end, however, it remained for the telegraph to dramatically cut down the time lag between the filing of a story and its appearance in a newspaper.

The New York Associated Press, using the wires of the Western Union Telegraph Co., soon dominated the news–gathering area of the newspaper business. And as Western Union expanded the range of its service, so too did the range of news-covering expand. By 1850, alert reporters in remote places were filing stories over Western Union wires at a great rate, and having their stories printed in a matter of days rather than weeks.

By 1900, the New York Associated Press had become the Associated Press, selling its services everywhere it could. It would soon be rivaled by United Press, set up by the Scripps newspaper chain, and later by both International News Service and the National Press Association, which was set up during the early years of

TREES USED AS EARLY TELEGRAPH POLES

the 20th century by the Hearst organization, a newspaper chain that had its beginnings during the mid-19th century in California.

The distribution of newspapers themselves, on the other hand, was not dealt with by an association of publishers but rather by the individual newspaper and a small army of newsboys.

Publisher Benjamin H. Day began the practice of sending out newsboys with papers that they had to pay for in advance—about 60-70 cents per hundred papers. The newsboy stood to make 30-40 cents profit on the hundred papers if he sold them all in one day. By 1835 the newsboys had built the *Sun's* circulation to close to 15,000 papers per day. Unsold newspapers were the

newsboys' loss.

The 1000 or more newsboys were homeless, ragged orphans, for the most part. Ranging in age from six to teens, they were toughened by the streets, the filthy slums and alleys they slept in. Many smoked, gambled, and drank their meager earnings away in the nearest saloon, where a jigger of whiskey could be had for three cents. In time, the newsboys bought their papers from horse-drawn wagons, often fighting and clawing each other for the torn bundles thrown from the backs of them.

In 1854, those newsboys who were lucky were cared for by the Children's Aid Society of New York in the Lodging-House, a dormitory-style establishment over

NEWSBOYS IN A SALOON

the offices of the *Sun* on Fulton Street. By the 1860's they were required to pay 5 cents for their bed and 4 cents for each meal. In the 1870's, Father John Christopher Drumgoole, a Catholic priest, began looking after the New York newsboys at St. Vincent's Newsboys Home on Warren Street. At the time of Father Drumgoole's death in 1888, St. Vincent's Newsboys Home was caring for about 300 boys.

By midcentury, the penny press had reached heights of circulation never known before in the newspaper industry. The United States, too, reached new heights of population, some 23 million, offering vast opportunities for the enterprising and industrious, not the least of whom were the penny press tycoons. Their papers

reached for success with sensational crime and sex stories, fantasies, hoaxes, and questionable product advertisements.

In 1850, the *Baltimore Sun* issued its first paper, while New York's *Sun* and *Herald* ceased to be penny papers. They raised their price to two cents per copy.

While New York City's leading newspapers were raising their prices, the city was playing host to a Swedish "nightingale." Jenny Lind, a soprano, recently arrived from Europe, gave her first American concert at Castle Garden, once a fort and soon to become an immigration station, an aquarium, and finally the site of a national monument at Battery Park in lower Manhattan. Miss Lind's manager was P. T. Barnum, a Connecticut entrepreneur who would go on to create a museum of oddities and a circus. In 1881 he merged his circus with that of J. A. Bailey to form the world-famous Barnum & Bailey Circus.

P. T. Barnum's first experience with self-advertisement came early in his life at the hands of the newspaper business. In 1831, the 21-year-old Barnum, anxious to be seen and heard, tried to sell articles to a Danbury, Connecticut, newspaper—his hometown paper. The paper turned him down. Barnum then bought a printing press and proceeded to insult the paper that refused to hire him. The paper sued Barnum for libel and had him tossed in jail for 60 days. While in jail, Barnum continued to publish his paper.

The people of Danbury were so impressed with Barnum's defiance and sass that upon his release he was greeted by a great crowd, speeches on his behalf and dealing with the freedom of the press, a marching brass band, and a salute from a cannon.

Any salute from a cannon would have seemed ominous in hindsight. America faced a crisis, with some states free and some states slave, and territories trying to decide how to be admitted into the union—free or slave. Already, some sketchy news had arrived from China telling about civil war there. During the period 1850-

P. T. BARNUM LEAVING JAIL

1864, the Taiping Rebellion—a civil war over European business presence in China—would bring death to some 30 million people and vast destruction to China.

World news was of particular interest to one of the New York *Tribune's* best reporters, Henry J. Raymond. In 1851, he left the paper and its boss, Horace Greeley, to create the *New York Daily Times,* later to be known simply as the *New York Times.* Raymond and his partners, George Jones and Edward B. Wesley, were bent on establishing a penny paper for people who did not read scandal, politics and commerce—not in equal measure—one or the other. Raymond wanted a balanced approach to the presentation of news. Sensationalism was not to be in the *Times'* character, not from the day of its birth, September 11, 1851. "The *Times* will seek to be conservative." wrote Raymond, "in such a way as shall best promote needful reform." Raymond's formula for improvement would be based on "Christianity and Republicanism."

Within weeks, the staid *New York Times* was soaring to success, hot on the heels of the *Herald* and *Sun* whose circulations ranged between 25,000 and 30,000 in a city of 700,000. Four of the six columns in the paper's first edition were devoted to news from England, Austria, Italy, Iceland and elsewhere abroad. The other two columns were devoted to local news dealing with an execution, a poisoning, a new steamboat line, the completion of a fountain in Washington Square, and this item:

"A Bloomer Costume made its appearance in Sixth-avenue day before yesterday. A crowd of "Conservatives" manifested their hostility to this progressive movement by derision. "New Ideas" are compelled to wage fierce battle in this world before they obtain recognition and favor. Two Bloomers appeared in Broadway and two in Washington square yesterday."

Competition was so keen, and newsgathering techniques were so primitive, that big city newspapers were not averse to stealing stories from one another. Not even the virtuous *Times* was aloof from such questionable practices.

In September, 1854, a westbound passenger ship from England, the *Arctic,* collided with another ship in the Atlantic and sank. Many lives were lost. The *New York Herald* learned of the sinking details first. It printed the story and locked it away for release at its usual release hour, 9 a.m.

The *Times* knew of the sinking, too, but had none of the details it knew the *Herald* had. The *Times'* night editor ordered one of his printers to steal a *Herald* paper. The printer broke into the *Herald's* locked offices and did what he was told to do. The *Times* editor worked all night rewriting the story and finally had it printed in time to have it on the streets at 8 a.m., one hour before the *Herald* knew what had happened.

Despite such an unseemly act, which was an acceptable activity in the newspaper business at midcentury, the reputation of the *New York Times* was beyond reproach both for the excellence of its journalism, and its behavior; and its circulation rose accordingly, helped by the populaton explosion in New York City—now about 800,000. There were about 30 million people elsewhere in America. And there was plenty of room for more newspapers to meet the demands of the American public for news and information of every description. Yet it remained for the *New York Times* to remain solidly committed to Raymond's credo of balanced news and reform. He sent Frederick Law Olmsted, who would soon design New York's Central Park, to the South to find out about slaves and slavery. In 1859, Raymond himself went to Europe to cover a war between Austria and France.

1859 was as eventful and as newsworthy a year as most of the other 20 previous years. The song "Dixie" was heard in New York City for the first time anywhere. America's first oil well began drilling in Pennsylvania. Englishman Charles Darwin startled the world with his book, *The Origin of Species,* a controversial work dealing with mankind's descendency from lower life forms rather than from Adam and Eve. And John Brown, a fiery abolitionist, heated up the slavery issue by capturing the United States Armory at Harpers Ferry, Virginia. He was caught by U.S. Marines, tried, and hanged at year's end. America was tumbling toward civil war.

III. 1860-1869

The intersection of Park Row, Nassau, and Spruce Streets near New York's City Hall was known as Printing-House Square. Printing-House Square was the heart of the newspaper business, not only in New York City but in America. There stood the buildings of the *Times,* the *Tribune,* and others, together with the printers and suppliers to the trade. The area was one of the busiest and noisiest in New York. During the spring and summer months, a variety of amusements attracted the leisure Sunday strollers. There were telescopes to look at the sky; machines to test the strength and quantity of air in one's lungs; and scales to keep track of one's weight.

PRINTING-HOUSE SQUARE

On the night of October 3, 1860, Printing-House Square was the scene of a mammoth demonstration staged by the Republican Party on behalf of the presidential candidacy of Abraham Lincoln and his running mate, Hannibal Hamlin. The torchlight parade that worked its way around the square carrying placards with the painting of a single eye and the words "wide awake," was not staged to gain the support of the *Times* and *Tribune,* which they already had.

Both papers were rooted in Republican politics, antislavery, pro-Union, and more or less pro-Lincoln. It was designed to catch the interest of the lower classes who were in the camp of Democratic politicians and those papers that supported Democratic politics. Anti-Lincoln and openly sympathetic to the Southern cause, the New York Democrats and their chief voice, the *Daily News* (not to be confused with the present-day *Daily News* founded in 1919), made the city a hotbed of Northern

THE DEMONSTRATION FOR LINCOLN AND HAMLIN

anti-Unionism.

None of this was lost on Henry J. Raymond of the *Times.* He was no mere sideline journalist. Raymond had already served a term as Lieutenant Governor of New York (1854-56) and was the Republican Party choice for governor, which he turned down. Later he would serve a term in Congress, run the Republican Party which he had helped to found in 1854*, and manage Lincoln's reelection campaign.

Lincoln was elected in November, 1860, without carrying New York City. He was inaugurated in March, 1861, and a month later was embroiled in the Civil War. For two years, the country bloodied itself from Mississippi to Pennsylvania. On January 1, 1863, Lincoln freed the slaves, many of whom headed north. In February, Lincoln called for the draft of 100,000 men to begin on Saturday, July 11th. Little did anyone suspect that that day would follow the Battle of Gettysburg by a week—a battle in which 7,000 Americans would die within 72 hours and 27,000 would be wounded. On Sunday, a mob sacked New York's draft headquarters at 46th Street and Third Avenue. The war had come to New York.

The mob was aroused and egged on by Democratic politicians including the Governor of New York, Horatio Seymour, and "copperhead" newspapers, which were named after the hostile copperhead snake. These were

---

*The Republican Party grew out of a coalition of the earlier Federalist, National Republican, Whig, and Free Soil Parties.

Northern Democratic newspapers that supported the South; however, not all Democratic papers were sympathetic to the pro-slavery South's secession from the Union.

The lower classes, many of whom were foreign born and had come to America to avoid the draft in their own countries, had voted Democratic, and resented the Republican sponsored draft law which had passed in March. Few of them had the $300 required to buy their way out of military service as the law allowed. Moreover, their lowly jobs were being threatened by the arrival of freed slaves willing to work at menial labor for even lower wages.

Between Sunday, July 12th, and Thursday, July 16th,

NEW YORK DRAFT RIOTS

wild mobs armed with weapons stolen from the Second Avenue Armory vented their discontent by burning, looting, and killing all over the city. They leveled the Colored Orphan Asylum on Fifth Avenue at 43rd Street. The children escaped unharmed but homeless. They picked Brooks Brothers Clothing Store on Cherry Street clean. They surged into Printing-House Square and headed straight for the building of the *New York Times*—a Lincoln paper. There, Henry J. Raymond waited with a machine gun and his fully armed employees, daring the enraged horde to enter the building. They never did. Instead, they took their frustration out across the street by wrecking Horace Greeley's *Tribune* — not so strong a Lincoln paper although loyal to the Union cause.

By the time the police, units of the 7th Regiment

quickly returned from Gettysburg, naval units, armed and deputized civilians, and West Point cadets had restored order, the loss of life and property was considerable. The city suffered $2,000,000 in property damage; more than 1,000 people had died, many of them blacks who were beaten to death, 18 of whom were lynched and left hanging from trees and lampposts. Thousands more were hurt.

Similar riots over the draft occurred elsewhere in northern cities, but none were as widespread, as bitter, and as damaging as those that occurred in New York. Governor Seymour pleaded, finally, with the people to obey the draft law while insisting it be tested in the courts. It never was. By August, New York youths were being peacefully drafted into the Union Army. Some 110,000 soldiers came from New York and helped save the Union.

As the war raged on, most newspapers sent correspondents to the battle areas to report on the progress of the fighting. None of these "war correspondents" were considered non-combatants. Although not legally enlisted into the military service, many of them joined the fighting. Some of them were used as aides to high ranking officers, thus putting them in a position to know more than they should have regarding the army's battle plans. In time, their newspapers not only printed long casualty lists on their front pages, but maps and enough information to weaken any element of surprise Union generals tried to maintain.

Some publications, although not strictly newspapers —*Frank Leslie's Illustrated Newspaper,* founded in 1855 and *Harper's Weekly* founded in 1857—sent artists and photographers to cover the war. Their works were reproduced (with the photos rendered as drawings) on the pages of every issue. It was the beginning of pictorial journalism. The two most outstanding figures in American art and photography whose images brought the war home to every American reader—the combined circulation of both periodicals was over 200,000 copies per issue—were Winslow Homer, painter, and Mathew B. Brady, photographer.

Until the war had ended, the copperhead press in any Northern city was an unsafe place to be. These newspapers were nearly the only voice the South had. Too many small Southern papers closed shop because their editors, owners, or pressmen had gone off to fight for the Confederacy. Papers still active could hardly find either the paper to print on or the ink, all of which came from suppliers in the North. And to make matters worse, Southern cities in federal hands had little to read since the military commanders closed down the papers. The fact is that Northern military commanders were so sensitive to criticism of their conduct of the war, that they would shut down any paper for its most innocent remarks, including Northern papers loyal to the Union, branding these papers "copperhead." In 1861, New York was plastered with signs proclaiming that "freedom of the press was subordinate to the interests of a nation." Many wondered, with justifiable fear, that even if the Union was saved, would it be saved intact—with the Constitution and its guarantees including the First Amendment: "Congress shall make no laws . . . abridging the freedom of speech, or of the press . . ."

At any rate, copperhead papers along with Democratic papers loyal to the Union, were constantly harassed by mobs of Northern sympathizers who seemed to demand absolute obedience to Lincoln and the Republicans, let alone to the nation and its promise. New York City had its *Daily News,* the *Weekly Day-Book,* the *World* and the *Copperhead.* Boston had its *Courier.* Philadelphia lived with the *Evening Journal,* the *Christian Observer,* and the *Age*—all copperheads. Every Northern state had its copperhead press as far away as Oregon.

The assassination of Abraham Lincoln in April, 1865, did little to ensure the hope that the wounds of the country could be quickly healed. Vice-President Andrew Johnson, a Democrat and southerner by birth, became President. Johnson's reconstruction policies quickly made him unpopular with an unforgiving Republican Congress. He felt that Southern leaders should help rebuild the South and that the South should not be left at the mercy of unsympathetic and unscrupulous North-erners. The Republican *New York Times*, as well as other moderate Republican papers, constantly criticized Johnson for his stubbornness and lack of imagination. Yet, the *Times* jumped to Johnson's defense when his opponents in Congress tried to have him impeached in 1868. Johnson was acquitted.

During those years, Nebraska became a state, Alaska became a United States Territory, and newspapers became so politically powerful that when President Johnson was asked to submit to an interview he could hardly refuse. He became the first American President to be interviewed by a newspaper, the St. Louis *Globe-Democrat*. Also, the Klu Klux Klan terrorized blacks throughout the South, and the typewriter was invented in Milwaukee, Wisconsin.

By 1869, some of the wounds of the Civil War had begun to heal—but slowly. The Klu Klux Klan had disbanded; Ulysses S. Grant had become the 18th President; the transcontinental railroad was completed; Henry J. Raymond was dead at 49; the *New York Times* was the largest and most respected newspaper in America; and Charles Anderson Dana, former managing editor of the New York *Tribune,* and Assistant Secretary of War, had become the new owner of the New York *Sun.* He would transform the listless *Sun* into a more dynamic, popular, outspoken, and successful enterprise.

IV. 1870-1899

The completion of the transcontinental railroad in 1869 opened the vast territories of the American West to opportunities so enormous that they were almost beyond the imagination of those willing to "go west." Between the end of the Civil War and the end of the century, the population of the United States leaped from

THE TRANSCONTINENTAL RAILROAD

about 40,000,000 to 75,000,000. The approximate number of newspapers in the country during the same period jumped from about 970 newspapers to a little more than 1600. But the jump in circulation during this same period was even more dramatic. Some 3,500,000 people read newspapers at the close of the Civil War. By the end of the century, nearly 8,500,000 people would be reading them. At the close of the Civil War, one out of every twelve Americans read a newspaper. By the end of the century one out of every nine read a paper.

Among the new papers were the San Francisco *Chronicle* founded in 1865; the Portland *Oregonian* whose first issue was in 1870; the *Chicago Daily News* in 1876, a paper founded by Victor Lawson and Melville Stone; Joseph Pulitzer's St. Louis *Post-Dispatch*, formed out of an auction sale at the Old Courthouse in St. Louis, Missouri, in 1878; E. W. Scripps' *Cleveland Press*, 1878; and in the 1880's the Kansas City *Star*, the Atlanta *Constitution*, and William Randolph Hearst's San Francisco *Examiner*.

Between 1870-1899, Americans became the best informed people on earth. Compulsory education in many places had taught most Americans how to read. The rapid growth of the newspaper business indicated a response to the American need to be informed on everything happening under the sun.

That need to know which was—and still is—part of the American instinct was rooted in fundamental ideas about freedom and civil liberty, the essential elements of independence and the strength of the nation. Moreover, there was nothing to prevent papers from exercising their right to print anything they pleased. And there was nothing to restrict the people from reading anything they could. All this was guaranteed by the First Amendment.

The news was always exciting, interesting, and breathless enough to keep the reading public on the edge of their chairs day after day. And the leading events of the last third of the century made enough anxious readers to firmly establish the .power of the press as nearly a branch of government with influence over every aspect of economic, political, and social life.

In 1871, Chicago was destroyed by fire. A month later, reporter Henry Morton Stanley of the New York *Tribune* found missionary-explorer David Livingstone in central Africa. Livingstone had no idea that he was missing. It was the paper's owner, James Gordon Bennett, who was curious to know if the long absent and unheard from Livingstone was dead or alive.

In 1874, New York City's most powerful politician, William "Boss" Tweed, went to jail for fraud and corruption. It was the investigative reporting of the *New York Times* that helped put him there.

Three unrelated events happened in 1876 to make headlines everywhere: George Armstrong Custer and his 7th Cavalry troopers were massacred by Sioux warriors led by Chief Crazy Horse at the Battle of the Little Big Horn in Montana; "Wild Bill" Hickok was shot in the back by Jack McCall in Deadwood, South Dakota (McCall was hanged for the deed); and Samuel J. Tilden received more votes for the presidency than Rutherford B. Hayes but lost the election. Republican Hayes had received more electoral college votes.

In 1878, telephones went into commercial service with the opening of a telephone exchange in New Haven, Connecticut. The telephone, together with the telegraph, made news-gathering techniques more efficient and the printing of news received over the "wires" almost immediate.

In 1881, President James A. Garfield was assassinated in a Washington, D.C., railroad station.

In 1883, President Chester Alan Arthur opened the Brooklyn Bridge, the world's longest suspension bridge. Twenty workmen died in its building, and six days after the opening ceremony twelve people were trampled to death in a panic that resulted from a rumor that the bridge was collapsing.

Labor battles in Chicago over an eight hour work day led to the Haymarket riots of 1886. Seven policemen were killed by a bomb. Scores more were injured. Later that year the American Federation of Labor was founded at Columbus, Ohio. Also in 1886, Apache Indian Chief Geronimo and his followers surrendered to U.S. Army troops.

In 1888, some 400 people died in the Great Blizzard, including Father John Christopher Drumgoole, who befriended the newsboys of New York. And in the following year, more than 2,000 lost their lives in the Johnstown, Pennsylvania, floods.

In 1890, the Battle of Wounded Knee—the last battle between Indians and the U.S. Army—took place in South Dakota. And in the East, Ellis Island opened as the new immigration station—the gateway to America for the millions of European immigrants who were swelling the country's population.

A revolution took place in Cuba in 1895. Marconi patented his radio wireless in 1896. And the United States went to war with Spain in 1898.

IMMIGRANTS ARRIVED BY THE MILLIONS

The growth of the newspaper industry during the last third of the 19th century was characterized by more independent journalism—a journalism free of political control, not always tied to political parties, party issues, politicians, and loyalties. One such newspaper, the *Washington Post* in Washington, D.C., which was founded in 1877 as a Democratic paper, became independent of party politics within ten years. Also, more and more pictures appeared in newspapers: sketches, drawings, cartoons, and diagrams. Photographs were hardly seen in papers, although photographic processes to reproduce pictures found their first commercial uses in America in 1880. And finally, groups of papers were coming under the control of individuals. The rise of newspapers chains

had begun.

One of the leaders in the movement to make newspapers more responsive to issues and the public was Joseph Pulitzer, whose St. Louis *Post-Dispatch* became a respected midwest paper. In 1883, Pulitzer bought the New York *World* and promoted it into being a major paper with excellent world-wide news coverage—America's chief spokesman and sounding board for liberal ideas, the voice of the Democratic Party, and a crusader for reform. Pulitzer was not above doing promotional stunts to increase his papers' circulation. In 1890, he sent reporter Elizabeth Cochran, alias Nellie Bly, around the world in a race against Jules Verne's storybook character Phileas Fogg, the hero of *Around the World in Eighty Days*. Nellie did it in 72 days.

Among the leaders in acquiring numerous newspapers to form large "chains" were the Scripps family, who were scattered throughout the Midwest, and William Randolph Hearst, a Californian.

Beginning chiefly with Edward Wyllis Scripps' founding of the *Cleveland Press* in 1878, the all too numerous Scripps family members under "E.W." 's leadership would eventually control more than 30 newspapers around the country. And this they did first as a Scripps organization, then in successive stages as the Scripps-McCrae League, the Scripps-Canfield League, and the Scripps-Howard League. Eventually, in 1931, Scripps-Howard bought Joseph Pulitzer's New York *World* and merged it with their own New York *Evening Telegram* to form the *New York World-Telegram,* which in 1950 acquired the *Sun* to become the *New York World-Telegram and Sun* before going out of business altogether a few years later.

Beginning with the San Francisco *Examiner* in 1885, William Randolph Hearst, son of a wealthy miner and United States Senator, went on to build a newspaper-magazine empire. It would not be until the 20th century, however, that the Hearst organization would include the International News Service*—a direct competitor to both the newly formed Associated Press and United Press†—and the magazines *House Beautiful, Good Housekeeping,* and *Harper's Bazaar,* among others.

In 1895, 10 years after he had made the *Examiner* a great financial success, Hearst bought the *New York Journal.* His immediate aim was to outdistance Pulitzer's *World* in popularity and circulation. The competition between the two newspapers was as fierce as it was sly, creating a brand of sensational journalism that was soon called "yellow journalism."

The term "yellow journalism" began with the comics. Cartoons were not altogether new to newspaper publishing. Political and socially satirical cartoons began appearing regularly in the 1830's, both in America and

---

*founded by Hearst in 1909

†the AP was formed out of the New York Associated Press and other news gathering services in 1900. UP was founded by the Scripps organization in 1907.

in Europe. The first political cartoon—a 13-part rattle-snake with the motto "Join or Die"—and attributed to Benjamin Franklin, appeared in the anti-British Colonial American press of 1774. However, no cartoon seemed to capture such wide public attention as a humorous drawing that appeared from time to time in the *World's* eight pages of Sunday comics. The appearance of a Sunday supplement of comics in 1894 was a new idea. The drawing called "Hogan's Alley" was the brainchild of Ohioan Richard Felton Outcault. The page-wide comic dealt with tenement life.

When the cartoon first appeared it was printed in black and white. In 1896, the *World* provided another "first." It printed half of the comics in color. A brilliant yellow was the most outstanding feature and it adorned the dress-like costume of the central figure in "Hogan's Alley." The cartoon was renamed "The Yellow Kid." It was an instant success and drove the circulation of the *World* within reach of the *Journal*.

William Randolph Hearst, not one easily put down, and not one to let opportunity slide by his bank roll, offered the staff of the *World's* Sunday supplement enough money so that they switched papers. Now they all worked for the *Journal*, including Outcault and his "Yellow Kid." Moreover, the *Journal* began printing its eight page Sunday comic supplement entirely in color.

Pulitzer, not to be outdone by his rival, and stunned by the defection of his carefully chosen staff, hired artist

George B. Luks to draw "The Yellow Kid" for the *World*. In 1896, New Yorkers had two "The Yellow Kid" cartoons every week. "The Yellow Kid" became a symbol of the sensational brand of news that characterized the circulation war between Hearst's *Journal* and Pulitzer's *World*. Other newspapers, chiefly the new York *Sun*, began referring to the *World* and *Journal* as New York's "yellow press," and the type of journalism practiced by the papers as "yellow kid journalism" or plain "yellow journalism." In no time, any type of sensational journalism regardless of the subject matter was known as "yellow."

THE YELLOW KID

The *Journal* and the *World* took their private war into the field of foreign affairs, turning their sights on unrest in Cuba. The two papers printed screaming accounts of terrible deeds of oppression that were being perpetrated on the Cuban people by the Spanish colonial government. The papers played on the sympathy of the American people for the underdog by printing accounts—many of them untrue or exaggerated—of Cuban misery under the Spanish yoke. The papers also appealed to those Americans who always thought that Cuba should have been American property, by agitating for American intervention in Cuban affairs. In effect, the two papers were creating a crisis environment that could lead to disaster. There was a continuous revolution in Cuba to add credence to the howling of the *Journal* and the *World*.

THE U.S.S. *MAINE*

Then pro-Spanish mobs rioted in Havana. In January, 1898, the U.S.S. *Maine* arrived in Havana harbor to protect American lives. In February, the *Maine* blew up. Two hundred and sixty members of her crew were killed. America blamed Spain. With the cry "Remember the *Maine*", President McKinley asked for a declaration of war from the Congress. He got it on April 25, 1898.

Spain lost the war. Cuba became independent. Spain ceded Puerto Rico and Guam to the United States, and the Philippine Islands were transferred to the U.S. in return for $20,000,000. The peace treaty between Spain and the United States was concluded in Paris in December, 1898, and ratified by the Congress two months later.

During the circulation battles between New York's *Journal* and *World,* the *New York Times* had slipped from public interest. The *Journal* and *World* had cap-

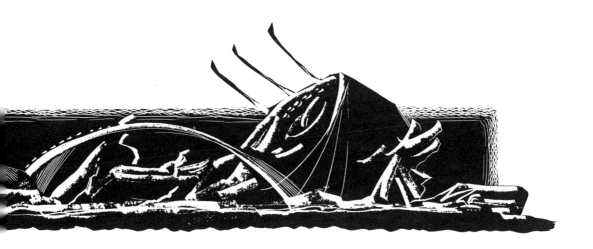

tured most of the attention of the buying public along with the *Sun*. As the headlines of these rival papers enlarged and thickened, and as their printing of color intensified, together with increased use of illustrations of every description, including melodramatic "X-marks-the-spot" diagrams of insignificant but sensational murders, the *Times*—the colorless, pictureless *Times*—looked old, tired, and stale. Its circulation dropped so low that it seemed as if the once proud paper would pass into oblivion, overwhelmed by a noisier press and public.

Near bankruptcy in 1896, the *New York Times* received a second chance. A new management team headed by a former Tennessee newsboy, Adolph S. Ochs, took on the job of reviving the paper. Eventually, under Och's direction, the *Times* would outlive its rivals and once again establish its supremacy as America's leading newspaper.

It remained for Ochs to outline the example of excellence in journalism—an example which the *New York Times* scrupulously observed during his 38-year tenure—which won over the public while establishing an ethical standard for all newspaper publishing:

" . . . to give the news impartially, without fear or favor . . . to make the columns . . . a forum for the consideration of all questions of public importance and . . . to invite intelligent discussion from all shades of opinion."

60

Index